PARTY CAKES

Publications International, Ltd.
www.pilcookbooks.com

D1060696

Pictured on the front cover *(clockwise from top left):* Little Lamb Cakes *(page 44),* School Daze *(page 8),* Surprise Package Cupcakes *(page 78)* and Dump Truck Cake *(page 40).*
Pictured on the back cover *(top to bottom):* Beautiful Butterflies *(page 24),* Lemon-Orange Party Cake *(page 82)* and Colorful Caterpillar Cupcakes *(page 46).*

ISBN-13: 978-1-60553-120-5
ISBN-10: 1-60553-120-0

Manufactured in China.

8 7 6 5 4 3 2 1

Preparation/Cooking Times: Preparation times are based on the approximate amount of time required to assemble the recipe before cooking, baking, chilling or serving. These times include preparation steps such as measuring, chopping and mixing. The fact that some preparations and cooking can be done simultaneously is taken into account. Preparation of optional ingredients and serving suggestions is not included.

Publications International, Ltd.
www.pilcookbooks.com

CONTENTS

· · · ·

LITTLE TIKES

····

Crayon Craze

1 package (about 18 ounces) cake mix, any flavor, plus
    ingredients to prepare mix
2 containers (16 ounces each) white frosting
    Gold, green, red, yellow, orange and blue food coloring
2 flat-bottomed ice cream cones

1. Prepare and bake cake mix according to package directions for 13×9-inch cake. Cool completely.

2. Measure 4½ inches down long sides of cake; draw line across top of cake with toothpick to create 9×4½-inch rectangle. Using toothpick line as guide, carefully cut halfway through cake (about 1 inch). (Do not cut all the way through cake.)

3. Split cake in half horizontally from 9-inch side just to cut made at 4½-inch line. Remove 9×4½×1-inch piece of cake; discard. Round edges of 9-inch side to resemble top of crayon box as shown in photo.

4. Tint 1 container frosting gold. Tint 1 cup frosting green. Divide remaining frosting into 4 parts (scant ¼ cup each). Tint one part red, one yellow, one orange and one blue. Frost entire cake with gold frosting. Using medium writing tip and green frosting, pipe "CRAYONS" on cake. Pipe stripes, triangles and decorative borders on crayon box as shown in photo.

5. Gently cut ice cream cones in half vertically with serrated knife. Frost each cone half different color (red, yellow, orange and blue). Place frosted cones on cake, just below rounded edge, to resemble crayon tips.

Makes 16 to 18 servings

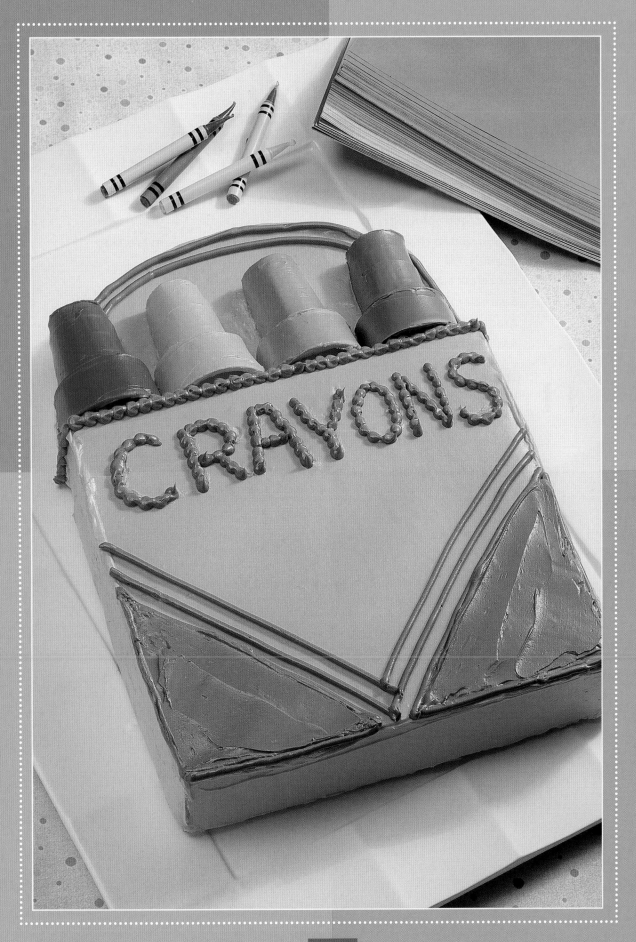

School Daze

1 (13×9-inch) cake

1 (19×13-inch) cake board, cut in half crosswise and covered, or large platter

1½ cups prepared white frosting or Buttercream Frosting (page 22)

Yellow food coloring

¾ cup prepared chocolate frosting or Chocolate Buttercream Frosting (page 34)

2 chocolate sandwich cookies

Bear-shaped graham crackers

Assorted color decorating gels

Assorted candies and black licorice twists

1. Trim top of cake to make level. Using diagram as guide, draw school bus pattern on 13×9-inch piece of waxed paper. Cut pattern out and place on cake. Cut out school bus; discard scraps. Place on prepared cake board.

2. Tint white frosting yellow. Frost entire cake with yellow frosting.

3. Frost bottom part of bus with chocolate frosting as shown in photo, reserving small portion for piping. Use 1 chocolate sandwich cookie as each wheel.

4. Using medium writing tip and chocolate frosting, pipe windows and door onto bus.

5. Decorate bear-shaped crackers with decorating gels; place in windows and door. Pipe and fill in stop sign with decorating gels. Decorate bus with candies and licorice as shown in photo.

Makes 12 to 16 servings

Tip: If you're not very experienced with piping frosting, you may want to draw the windows and the door on the bus with a toothpick before piping. Having lines to follow will make the job easier (and less messy).

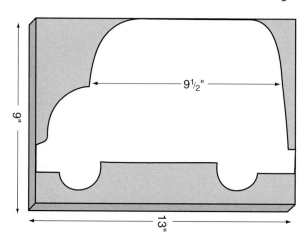

Circus Train Mini Cakes

1 package (about 18 ounces) super-moist chocolate fudge cake mix
1⅓ cups water
½ cup vegetable oil
3 eggs
2 containers (16 ounces each) chocolate frosting
2 round candy wafers
Candy-coated chocolates
Licorice snap
Round mints, assorted colors
Iced animal crackers

1. Preheat oven to 350°F. Spray 6 (4×2×2-inch) disposable foil mini loaf pans and 1 disposable foil cupcake cup with nonstick cooking spray.

2. Beat cake mix, water, oil and eggs in large bowl with electric mixer at low speed 30 seconds. Scrape down side of bowl; beat at medium speed 2 minutes or until batter is mixed well.

3. Pour batter into prepared pans, filling two-thirds full. Bake 13 to 15 minutes or until toothpick inserted into centers comes out clean. Cool 10 minutes in pans on wire racks. Remove to racks; cool completely.

4. Place engine car at front edge of large platter. Line up train cars behind engine. Frost cars, using bottom of each loaf as top. Place cupcake, upside down, on top of engine car, lining it up with rear of car; frost cupcake.

5. Use wafers and candies for eyes, nose and mouth. Use licorice snap for smokestack. Place mints on each car for wheels. Place another mint on last car for taillight. Place animal crackers on top of cars.   *Makes 12 servings*

Alphabet Block Cake

2 (8-inch) square cakes*
1 cup (2 sticks) butter, softened
⅓ cup shortening
8 cups (2 pounds) powdered sugar, sifted, divided
½ cup plus 2 tablespoons milk, divided
1 teaspoon vanilla
Blue food coloring
Yellow food coloring
1 cake board (19 × 14 inches)
2½ cups jelly, any flavor, melted
Pink decorating icing
Letter-shaped cookie cutters
Assorted colored candies
Colored sprinkles

Use your favorite cake recipe or package mix; follow baking instructions for two 8-inch square cakes.

1. Trim tops and edges of cakes to make level and of equal size. Cut each cake horizontally into 2 layers.

2. Beat together butter and shortening in large bowl with electric mixer at medium speed. Beat in 4 cups powdered sugar, ½ cup milk and vanilla at low speed until smooth. Add remaining 4 cups powdered sugar; beat until light and fluffy. Add more milk, 1 tablespoon at a time, as needed for good spreading consistency. Tint ¾ cup frosting pastel blue and ¾ cup frosting pastel yellow; reserve 3 cups white frosting.

3. Cut cake board into 2 (7 × 7-inch) squares. Stack and wrap in foil. Cut remaining board into 6½-inch square. Place 1 cake layer on 7-inch boards; frost top with ¾ cup white frosting. Top with second cake layer; frost top with ¾ cup white frosting.

4. Place 6½-inch board on top of cake. Top with third cake layer. Frost top with ¾ cup white frosting. Top with fourth cake layer.

5. Cover top and sides of cake with light coating of jelly to seal in crumbs. Frost top and sides of cake with blue, yellow and white frosting, alternating colors.

6. Outline edges of cake with pink icing. Using letter cookie cutters, make outlines on block. Using writing tip and remaining frosting, pipe outline of letters. Fill with candies and sprinkles.

7. Slice and serve top 2 layers of cake first. To serve bottom section, remove cake board before slicing.   *Makes 32 to 36 servings*

Tip: Personalize cake by using favorite colors and candies and spelling out child's name or initials.

Look Who's One

1 (13×9-inch) cake

1 (19×13-inch) cake board, cut in half crosswise and covered

1½ cups prepared white frosting or Buttercream Frosting (page 22)

Yellow food coloring

Assorted colored candies

1. Trim top of cake to make level. Using diagram as guide, draw number 1 pattern on 13×9-inch piece of waxed paper. Cut pattern out and place on cake. Cut out number 1; place on prepared cake board.

2. Tint frosting yellow. Frost cake with yellow frosting.

3. Decorate with assorted candies as desired. *Makes 12 to 16 servings*

Tip: Try using a novelty cake mix instead of a plain one for a change of pace. Mixes that add swirls or confetti to the batter provide an unexpected bit of color when you cut into the cake.

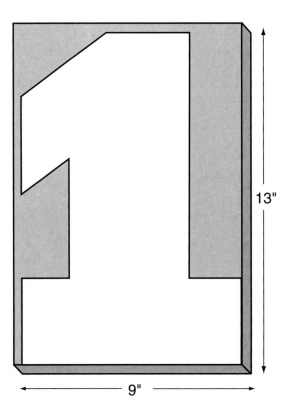

Carousel Cake

1 (10-inch) bundt cake
1 container (16 ounces) white frosting, softened
Orange food coloring
Assorted animal-shaped cookies
Decorating gel (optional)
Assorted candies and decors
Colored or striped drinking straws
Paper Carousel Roof (instructions follow)

1. Place cake on large platter.

2. Tint frosting orange. Frost cake with orange frosting, allowing frosting to drip down side of cake.

3. Outline animal-shaped cookies with decorating gel, if desired. Arrange cookies on top of cake. Press candies and decors lightly into frosting.

4. Place straws around cake to support carousel roof; carefully set roof on top of straws.
                                                                  Makes 14 to 16 servings

Paper Carousel Roof: Cut out 7½-inch circle from 8½×11-inch sheet of construction paper. Cut a second 7½-inch circle from construction paper in another color and fold into 8 wedges. Carefully cut out 4 wedges; glue them onto first circle of paper so colors alternate. Cut one slit from outer edge of circle to center; tape cut edges together to form carousel roof.

SUPER GIRLY

••••

Ballet Slippers

1 package (about 18 ounces) white cake mix with pudding in the mix, plus ingredients to prepare mix

1 container (16 ounces) white frosting

Red food coloring

1 tube (4¼ ounces) pink decorating icing

Pink ribbon

1. Prepare cake mix and bake in 13×9-inch baking pan according to package directions. Cool completely in pan on wire rack. Remove from pan; wrap in plastic wrap. Freeze overnight.

2. Cut frozen cake in half lengthwise, then cut each half into ballet slipper shape using photo as guide; discard scraps. Arrange slippers on serving platter.

3. Reserve ⅓ cup white frosting. Tint remaining frosting with red food coloring to desired shade of pink. Frost slippers entirely with pink frosting.

4. Frost center of each slipper with reserved white frosting, leaving 1 inch on each side and 3 inches at toe. To add texture, lightly press cheesecloth into frosting and lift off. Outline soles and centers of slippers with pink icing. Tie ribbon into two bows; place on toes of slippers before serving.   *Makes 12 to 16 servings*

Individual Flower Pot Cakes

18 (2½×4-inch) sterilized unglazed terra cotta flower pots*
1 package (about 18 ounces) dark chocolate cake mix, plus
   ingredients to prepare mix
1 package (12 ounces) semisweet chocolate chips
8 to 10 chocolate sandwich cookies, broken
1 container (16 ounces) chocolate frosting
   Green drinking straws
   Lollipops
   Decorating icing and assorted candies
   Spearmint leaves and gummy worms

Wash and dry pots. Place in 350°F oven 3 hours to sterilize. Cool completely.

1. Preheat oven to 350°F. Grease flower pots generously; line bottoms with greased parchment paper.

2. Prepare cake mix according to package directions; stir in chocolate chips.

3. Place pots in standard (2½-inch) muffin cups; divide batter among pots, filling half full. Bake 35 to 40 minutes or until toothpick inserted into centers comes out clean. Remove pots from muffin pans; cool completely on wire racks.

4. Place cookies in food processor; process using on/off pulses until coarse crumbs form.

5. Frost tops of cakes with chocolate frosting. Sprinkle cookie crumbs over frosting to resemble dirt. Push straws into flower pots for stems; trim straws to different heights with scissors.

6. Decorate lollipops with decorating icing and assorted candies. Insert lollipops into straw stems. Decorate pots with spearmint leaves and gummy worms.

Makes 18 mini cakes

Princess Doll

4 cups cake batter

1 (8-inch) round cake

1 (10-inch) round cake board, covered, or large plate

3 cups Buttercream Frosting (recipe follows), colored peach

1 cup Base Frosting (page 23, optional)

1 doll body and head*

   Pastel miniature marshmallows

   Edible candy pearls

   Small chocolate nonpareil candies

*Doll body and head can be purchased from stores carrying cake decorating supplies, or use doll with legs removed or covered in plastic wrap.

1. Preheat oven to 350°F. Grease and flour 2-quart ovenproof bowl. Pour 4 cups cake batter into prepared bowl. Bake 1 hour and 15 minutes or until toothpick inserted into center comes out clean. Cool 15 minutes in bowl; loosen edge. Invert onto wire rack; cool completely.

2. Trim flat side of bowl cake and top of round cake. Trim round cake even with bowl cake. Place round cake on prepared cake board. Frost top with some of the peach frosting. Place bowl cake, flat-side down, on top of frosting. Frost entire cake with Base Frosting to seal in crumbs, if desired.

3. Make small V-shaped hole in center of cake; insert doll in hole. Frost cake and doll torso with remaining peach frosting.

4. Decorate skirt with flattened marshmallows, candy pearls and chocolate nonpareil candies. To serve, remove doll and slice cake into wedges.

Makes 14 to 18 servings

Buttercream Frosting

6 cups powdered sugar, sifted, divided

¾ cup (1½ sticks) butter, softened

¼ cup shortening

6 to 8 tablespoons milk, divided

1 teaspoon vanilla

Beat 3 cups powdered sugar, butter, shortening, 4 tablespoons milk and vanilla in large bowl with electric mixer at low speed until smooth. Add remaining

3 cups powdered sugar; beat until light and fluffy, adding more milk,
1 tablespoon at a time, as needed for good spreading consistency.

Makes about 3½ cups

Base Frosting

  3 cups powdered sugar, sifted
½ cup (1 stick) butter, softened
¼ cup milk
½ teaspoon vanilla

Beat powdered sugar, butter, milk and vanilla in large bowl with electric mixer
at low speed until smooth. Add more milk, 1 teaspoon at a time, as needed for
thin consistency.

Makes about 2 cups

Beautiful Butterflies

1 package (about 18 ounces) spice cake mix, plus ingredients to prepare mix

1 container (16 ounces) cream cheese or white chocolate frosting

Food coloring, any color

8 to 10 round chocolate wafer cookies, cut in half

Pastel-colored candy-coated chocolate pieces

Confetti sprinkles

Decorating sugar

1. Preheat oven to 350°F. Grease and flour two 8-inch round cake pans.

2. Prepare cake mix according to package directions. Spread batter evenly in prepared pans. Bake 30 minutes or until toothpick inserted into centers comes out clean. Cool cakes completely.

3. Tint frosting desired color. Place one cake layer on serving platter; spread with ½ cup frosting. Top with second cake layer; frost top and side of cake with remaining frosting.

4. Arrange 2 wafer cookie halves on cake about ½ inch apart, cut sides facing out, to create butterfly. Repeat with remaining cookies. Place 2 chocolate pieces in center of each butterfly as shown in photo. Use remaining chocolate pieces to decorate bottom edge of cake. Arrange sprinkles to resemble antennae on each butterfly. Sprinkle cake with sugar.   *Makes 12 servings*

To tint frosting properly, add a small amount of desired food coloring; stir until completely combined. Gradually add more coloring until the desired shade of frosting is reached.

Sleepover Cake

1 package (about 18 ounces) cake mix, any flavor, plus ingredients to prepare mix

1 container (16 ounces) white frosting

Pink food coloring

2 individual sponge cakes with cream filling

Colored sprinkles

4 large marshmallows

Assorted candies

Red, black or brown licorice strings

4 chocolate peanut butter cups (milk and/or white chocolate)

White decorating icing

2 packages (6 feet each) bubble gum tape (pink and/or green)

Bear-shaped graham crackers

1. Prepare and bake cake mix according to package directions in 13×9-inch pan. Cool cake 10 minutes in pan on wire rack. Remove from pan; cool completely.

2. Tint frosting pink. Place cake on serving platter; frost top and sides with pink frosting.

3. Cut sponge cakes in half lengthwise. Arrange sponge cakes, cut sides down, on top of frosted cake. Frost sponge cakes; sprinkle with colored sprinkles.

4. Flatten marshmallows by pressing down firmly with palm of hand. Arrange marshmallows at top of snack cakes to resemble pillows. Attach assorted candies and licorice to peanut butter cups with icing to create eyes, lips and hair. Place decorated peanut butter cups on marshmallow pillows.

5. Unwind 1 bubble gum tape; arrange across cake at edge of peanut butter cups to form edge of blanket. Arrange second bubble gum tape around base of cake. Tuck bear-shaped graham crackers around blanket.

Makes 16 servings

Football Cake

1 package DUNCAN HINES® Moist Deluxe® Devil's Food Cake Mix

Decorator Frosting

> **¾ cup confectioners' sugar**
>
> **2 tablespoons shortening plus additional for greasing**
>
> **1 tablespoon cold water**
>
> **1 tablespoon non-dairy powdered creamer**
>
> **¼ teaspoon vanilla extract**
>
> **Dash salt**
>
> **1 container DUNCAN HINES® Creamy Home-Style Chocolate Frosting**

1. Preheat oven to 350°F. Grease and flour 10-inch round cake pan. Prepare cake following package directions for basic recipe. Bake at 350°F for 45 to 55 minutes or until toothpick inserted in center comes out clean.

2. For decorator frosting, combine confectioners' sugar, shortening, water, non-dairy powdered creamer, vanilla extract and salt in small bowl. Beat at medium speed with electric mixer 2 minutes. Add more confectioners' sugar to thicken or water to thin frosting as needed.

3. Cut 2-inch wide piece from center of cake; remove. Place cake halves together to make football shape as shown. Spread chocolate frosting on sides and top of cake. Place basketweave tip in pastry bag. Fill with decorator frosting. Make white frosting laces on football.   *Makes 12 to 16 servings*

Tip: If a 10-inch round pan is not available, make 2 football cakes by following package directions for baking with two 9-inch round cake pans.

Fun Fort

1 package (about 18 ounces) devil's food cake mix, plus ingredients to prepare mix

2 cups Chocolate Buttercream Frosting (recipe follows)

6 square chocolate-covered snack cakes

9 cream-filled wafer cookies

1 tube (4¼ ounces) chocolate decorating icing with tips

1 tube (4¼ ounces) white decorating icing with tips

1 tube (4¼ ounces) green decorating icing with tips

Sprinkles

Paper flag and plastic figurines (optional)

1. Prepare and bake cake mix in two 8-inch square baking pans according to package directions. Cool 15 minutes in pans on wire racks. Remove from pans; cool completely.

2. Place 1 cake layer upside down on serving platter; frost top. Place second layer upside down on first cake layer so cake top is completely flat. Frost top and sides. Place 1 square snack cake in each corner of large cake. Cut remaining 2 snack cakes in half diagonally; place 1 half cut side down on top of each snack cake in corners.

3. Attach wafer cookies to cake for fence posts, front gate and flagpole. Decorate fort with chocolate, white and green icings and sprinkles as desired. Attach flag to flagpole with chocolate icing and place figurines on top of cake, if desired.

Makes 12 servings

Chocolate Buttercream Frosting

6 cups powdered sugar, sifted, divided

1 cup (2 sticks) butter, softened

4 to 6 squares (1 ounce each) unsweetened chocolate, melted and cooled slightly

8 to 10 tablespoons milk, divided

1 teaspoon vanilla

Beat 3 cups powdered sugar, butter, melted chocolate, to taste, 6 tablespoons milk and vanilla in large bowl with electric mixer at low speed until smooth. Add remaining 3 cups powdered sugar; beat until light and fluffy, adding more milk, 1 tablespoon at a time, as needed for good spreading consistency.

Makes about 3½ cups

Toy Jeep

1 container (16 ounces) white frosting, divided
  Red and blue food coloring
1 frozen pound cake (10 ounces), thawed
¼ cup prepared chocolate frosting
2 individual sponge cakes with cream filling
½ graham cracker
  Edible silver dragées
  Black licorice strings
4 miniature chocolate-frosted doughnuts
4 sugar-coated gumdrops
4 plain gumdrops
2 pretzel rods

1. Reserve ½ cup white frosting; set aside. Tint remaining white frosting red. Place pound cake on serving plate; frost top and sides of cake with red frosting.

2. Blend ¼ cup white frosting and chocolate frosting in small bowl; mix well. Place sponge cakes, flat sides facing forward, across center and rear of pound cake to create seats; frost with light brown frosting. Cut small slit crosswise in front section of pound cake; slide graham cracker half into slit.

3. Tint remaining ¼ cup frosting light blue; frost graham cracker. Decorate with silver dragées and licorice to resemble windshield.

4. Press doughnuts into sides of cake to resemble wheels; add sugar-coated gumdrops for hubcaps. Attach plain gumdrops to jeep for headlights and taillights. Bend licorice strings; press into top of sponge cakes as shown in photo. Cut pretzels as needed and press onto front and rear of jeep to resemble bumpers.

Makes 10 servings

Touchdown!

1 package (about 18 ounces) cake mix, any flavor, plus ingredients to prepare mix

1 container (16 ounces) white frosting

Green food coloring

Assorted color decorating gels

1 square (2 ounces) almond bark

2 pretzel rods

4 thin pretzel sticks

Bear-shaped graham crackers

1. Prepare and bake cake mix according to package directions for 13×9-inch cake. Cool completely.

2. Tint frosting green. Frost entire cake with green frosting. Pipe field lines with white decorating gel.

3. Melt almond bark in tall glass according to package directions. Break off one fourth of each pretzel rod; discard shorter pieces. Break 2 pretzel sticks in half. Dip pretzels in melted almond bark, turning to coat completely and tapping off excess. Using pretzel rods for support posts, pretzel sticks for crossbars and pretzel stick halves for uprights, arrange pretzels in two goalpost formations on waxed paper; let stand until set. Carefully peel waxed paper from goalposts; arrange on each end of cake.

4. Meanwhile, decorate bear-shaped crackers with decorating gels; arrange on cake as desired.

Makes 16 to 20 servings

Dump Truck Cake

1 package (about 18 ounces) devil's food cake mix, plus ingredients to prepare mix

10 chocolate sandwich cookies, broken

3 containers (16 ounces each) white frosting

Red and yellow food coloring

Rectangular cake board

Assorted candy: round fruit jelly candies, rock candy and red licorice

6 miniature chocolate-frosted doughnuts

1. Preheat oven to 350°F. Grease 15×10-inch jelly-roll pan. Line with parchment paper; spray with nonstick cooking spray.

2. Prepare cake mix according to package directions. Spread batter evenly into prepared pan. Bake 20 minutes or until toothpick inserted into center comes out clean. Cool cake completely in pan on wire rack.

3. Meanwhile, place cookies in food processor or blender; process using on/off pulsing action until cookies resemble coarse crumbs. Set aside.

4. Lift cake from pan using parchment paper as aid. Trim ¼ inch off edges of cake using serrated knife. Cut cake into 4 equal sections (diagram A). Cut 3 inches off short end of 1 cake section. Wrap each section in plastic wrap; freeze several hours before frosting.

5. Tint 2 containers frosting red. Tint half container frosting yellow. Leave remaining half container frosting white. Remove cake layers from freezer;

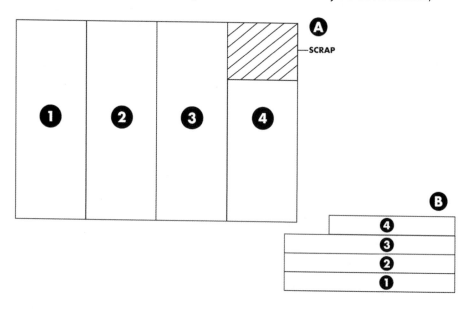

unwrap. Cut cake board to same size as bottom layer; wrap in foil. Place small amount of frosting on cake board to secure first cake layer; frost top of cake with red frosting. Continue stacking and frosting second and third layers.

6. Stack short layer on top of other layers so 1 end of cake has 4 layers and other has 3 (diagram B). Frost entire cake with remaining red frosting. Carefully place cake on large platter. Refrigerate cake to set.

7. Create windows with white frosting. Frost back of dump truck with yellow frosting as shown in photo. Using pastry bag fitted with plain tip, outline doors and grill with yellow frosting. Attach jelly candy headlights. Press doughnuts into sides of truck to resemble tires. Fill top of dump truck with cookie crumbs and accent with rock candy and licorice.

Makes 12 to 16 servings

Slam Dunk

1 (9-inch) round cake
1 (10-inch) round cake board, covered, or large plate
1¾ cups prepared white frosting
Orange and black food coloring
3 to 4 black licorice twists
Small clean sponge

1. Trim top of cake to make level. Place on prepared cake board.

2. Reserve ¼ cup frosting. Tint 1¼ cups frosting deep orange (rust) and remaining ¼ cup frosting black.

3. Frost entire cake with orange frosting.

4. Place licorice twists, end to end, around edge of cake to create rim of basketball hoop, trimming licorice as needed. Chill cake 15 minutes to set.

5. Press very slightly dampened clean sponge against top and side of cake to create dimpled surface resembling texture of basketball.

6. Using medium writing tip and black frosting, pipe line design on top of cake. Pipe net design on side of cake with reserved white frosting as shown in photo.

Makes 10 to 12 servings

> Trimming the tops of cake layers gives more professional results. Use a serrated knife long enough to cut across the top in one stroke. Use a gentle sawing motion as you cut through the cake.

CRAZY CRITTERS

····

Little Lamb Cakes

1 package (about 18 ounces) yellow cake mix, plus
    ingredients to prepare mix
1 container (16 ounces) vanilla frosting
15 large marshmallows
    Pink jelly beans or decorating candies
1 package (10½ ounces) mini marshmallows
    Black licorice string
44 mini chocolate chips

1. Preheat oven to 350°F. Line 22 standard (2½-inch) muffin cups with paper baking cups. Prepare cake mix according to package directions. Spoon batter into prepared muffin cups, filling two-thirds full.

2. Bake 18 to 22 minutes or until toothpick inserted into centers comes out clean. Cool cupcakes 10 minutes in pans on wire racks. Remove to racks; cool completely.

3. Frost cupcakes. Cut each large marshmallow crosswise into 3 pieces. Stretch pieces into oval shapes; arrange on cupcakes to resemble ears. Attach pink jelly bean to each ear with frosting.

4. Press mini marshmallows into frosting around edge of cupcakes. Cut jelly beans in half crosswise; cut licorice into ½-inch pieces. Create faces with mini chips for eyes, half jelly bean for nose and licorice for mouth.

Makes 22 cupcakes

Colorful Caterpillar Cupcakes

1 package (about 18 ounces) vanilla cake mix
1¼ cups water
3 eggs
⅓ cup vegetable oil
Assorted food coloring
Buttercream Frosting (page 22)
Assorted candies, candy-coated chocolates, red string licorice and lollipops
Gummy worms

1. Preheat oven to 350°F. Line 20 standard (2½-inch) muffin cups with paper baking cups.*

2. Beat cake mix, water, eggs and oil in large bowl with electric mixer at low speed 30 seconds. Beat at medium speed 2 minutes or until well blended. Divide batter between 5 bowls; tint each bowl with different color food coloring. Spoon batter into prepared muffin cups, filling three-fourths full.

3. Bake 15 to 18 minutes or until toothpick inserted into centers comes out clean. Cool cupcakes 10 minutes in pans on wire racks. Remove to racks; cool completely.

4. Prepare Buttercream Frosting. Set aside 2 cupcakes for caterpillar head.

5. Frost remaining cupcakes. Place 1 cupcake on its side towards one end of serving platter. Place second cupcake on its side next to first cupcake; arrange remaining cupcakes, alternating colors, in row to create body of caterpillar.

6. Frost 1 reserved cupcake; decorate with assorted candies, chocolates, licorice and lollipops to create face. Place plain cupcake at front of cupcake row for head. Top with face cupcake on its side; attach with frosting. Cut gummy worms into small pieces; attach to caterpillar body with frosting to create legs.

Makes 20 cupcakes

Use white paper baking cups to best show colors of caterpillar.

Big Cheek Bunny Cake

1 package (about 18 ounces) cake mix, any flavor, plus ingredients to prepare mix

Fluffy White Frosting (page 49)

1 (15×10-inch) cake board, covered, or large tray

2 cups shredded coconut, tinted pink*

2 coconut-covered cupcakes

Red string licorice

Assorted candies

To tint coconut, dilute a few drops of red food coloring with ½ teaspoon water in a large resealable food storage bag; add coconut. Seal the bag and shake well until evenly coated. If a deeper color is desired, add more diluted food coloring and shake again.

1. Preheat oven to 350°F. Prepare and bake cake mix according to package directions in two 8- or 9-inch round cake pans. Cool 10 minutes in pans on wire racks. Remove to racks; cool completely.

2. Meanwhile, prepare Fluffy White Frosting.

3. Cut out 3 cake pieces from 1 cake round as shown in diagram 1. Position cakes on prepared cake board as shown in diagram 2, connecting pieces with small amount of frosting. Frost cake with remaining frosting; sprinkle with coconut. Decorate with cupcakes, licorice and candies as desired.

Makes 12 servings

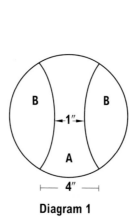

Diagram 1

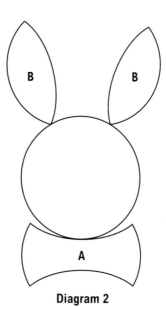

Diagram 2

Fluffy White Frosting

1 container (16 ounces) vanilla frosting

¾ cup marshmallow creme

Combine frosting and marshmallow creme in medium bowl; mix well.

Makes about 2 cups frosting

Speedy the Turtle

1 package (about 18 ounces) cake mix, any flavor, plus ingredients to prepare mix

1 (10-inch) round cake board, covered, or large plate

1¼ cups prepared white frosting

Green and brown food coloring

5 to 6 pecan swirl rolls

Assorted candies and red licorice string

4 walnut halves

1. Preheat oven to 350°F. Grease and flour 2½-quart ovenproof bowl and standard (2½-inch) muffin cups. Pour 4 cups cake batter into prepared bowl; pour remaining cake batter into muffin cups.

2. Bake cake 60 to 70 minutes and cupcakes 20 minutes or until toothpick inserted into centers comes out clean. Cool cake 15 minutes in bowl; loosen edge. Invert onto wire rack; cool completely.

3. Trim flat side of bowl cake. Place on prepared cake board, flat side down. Cut about one third off bottom of one cupcake. (Reserve remaining cupcakes for another use.)

4. Tint frosting olive green using green and brown food coloring.

5. Frost cake and cupcake with green frosting. Attach cupcake to cake with small amount of frosting to form turtle head as shown in photo.

6. Cut pecan swirl rolls into ¼-inch-thick slices. Place slices close together to form rows until entire body of turtle is covered. Press candy into center of each pecan roll slice.

7. Decorate face with assorted candies and licorice. Arrange walnut halves, flat sides down, to resemble feet as shown in photo.

Makes 14 to 18 servings

Lucy the Ladybug

  1 package (about 18 ounces) chocolate cake mix, plus ingredients to prepare mix

1½ cups prepared white frosting

    Red food coloring

  1 cup prepared chocolate frosting

12 chocolate discs

  2 candy-coated chocolate pieces

  1 string black licorice, cut into 6 pieces

  1 ring red gummy candy

1. Preheat oven to 350°F. Grease and flour 2-quart ovenproof bowl.*

2. Prepare cake mix according to package directions. Pour 4 cups cake batter into prepared bowl.**

3. Bake 1 hour and 15 minutes or until toothpick inserted into center comes out clean. Cool 15 minutes in bowl; loosen edge. Invert onto wire rack; cool completely.

4. Tint white frosting red. Mark a semicircle about 3 inches from edge of cake for head as shown in photo. Frost remaining cake with red frosting. Frost ladybug head with chocolate frosting.

5. Using medium writing tip and chocolate frosting, pipe line down center from head to other edge. Arrange chocolate discs on body to make polka dots. Place chocolate pieces in center of face to make eyes. Place 3 black licorice pieces above each chocolate piece to make eyelashes. Cut gummy ring in half; place under eyes to make mouth.   *Makes 14 to 18 servings*

*If using a glass bowl, reduce the oven temperature to 325°F.

**Use remaining batter for cupcakes.

Peanut

2 (8-inch) round cake layers
1 (14×10-inch) cake board, covered, or large platter
2 containers (16 ounces each) white frosting
  Pink food coloring
1 flat-bottomed ice cream cone
2 gumdrops
  Red licorice string
  Peanut-shaped peanut butter cookies

1. Trim tops of cakes to make level. Cut one cake layer in half.

2. Place round cake on prepared cake board. Place cake halves on either side of round cake to form ears as shown in photo.

3. Tint frosting pink. Frost entire cake with pink frosting. Cut off top of ice cream cone with serrated knife. Frost cone with pink frosting; place on round cake to form trunk.

4. Decorate elephant with gumdrops, pieces of licorice and peanut butter cookies as shown in photo.

Makes 16 to 20 servings

> Using store-bought cookies and candies is an easy way to be creative and decorate a party cake. You can get maximum effect with minimal effort.

Slinky the Snake

2 packages (about 18 ounces each) cake mix, any flavor, plus
    ingredients to prepare mix
2 containers (16 ounces each) white frosting
    Green food coloring
1 cup semisweet chocolate chips
    Red fruit leather
    Assorted candies

1. Prepare and bake cake mixes according to package directions for two 12-cup bundt cakes. Cool completely.

2. Cut each bundt cake in half. Position each half, end to end, to form one long serpentine shape as shown in photo. Attach pieces with frosting.

3. Tint frosting green. Frost top of cakes with green frosting, spreading frosting about halfway down sides of cakes.

4. Place chocolate chips in small resealable food storage bag. Microwave on MEDIUM (50%) 20 seconds. Knead bag several times; microwave 20 seconds more until chocolate is melted. Cut off tiny corner of bag; pipe diamond pattern on back of snake as shown in photo.

5. Cut out tongue from fruit leather; attach to snake head. Decorate face and back of snake with assorted candies.

Makes 32 to 36 servings

Panda Cupcakes

1 package (about 18 ounces) yellow cake mix, plus ingredients to prepare mix

1 container (16 ounces) vanilla frosting

44 chocolate discs*

44 small chocolate nonpareil candies

8 ounces semisweet chocolate, chopped, *or* 1½ cups semisweet chocolate chips

44 white candy flower sprinkles

22 red jelly beans

*Chocolate discs are available at many gourmet, craft and baking supply stores. Large chocolate nonpareil candies may be substituted.

1. Preheat oven to 350°F. Line 22 standard (2½-inch) muffin cups with paper baking cups. Prepare cake mix according to package directions. Spoon batter into prepared muffin cups, filling two-thirds full.

2. Bake 18 to 22 minutes or until toothpick inserted into centers comes out clean. Cool cupcakes 10 minutes in pans on wire racks. Remove to racks; cool completely.

3. Frost cupcakes. Arrange 2 chocolate discs on edge of each cupcake for ears. Attach 1 nonpareil candy to each ear with frosting.

4. Place semisweet chocolate in small resealable food storage bag. Microwave on HIGH about 1½ minutes or until chocolate is melted, kneading bag every 30 seconds. Cut very small hole in corner of bag; pipe kidney shapes for eyes. Place candy sprinkle on each eye. Place jelly bean between eyes for nose. Pipe mouth with melted chocolate. *Makes 22 cupcakes*

SEASONAL SENSATIONS

••••

Lucky Shamrock Cake

1 package (about 18 ounces) white cake mix, plus ingredients to prepare mix

1 container (16 ounces) white frosting

2 tubes (4¼ ounces each) green decorating icing with decorating tips

Irish-themed candy decorations

1. Prepare and bake cake mix according to package directions for two 9-inch round cakes. Cool cakes completely.

2. Place one cake layer on serving plate; spread with frosting. Top with second cake layer; frost top and side of cake.

3. Use green icing to create blades of grass around base of cake. Decorate with candy decorations as desired.   *Makes 10 servings*

Check your craft store or supermarket for candy decorations. Keep your eye out for after-holiday sales and pick up extras. They have a long shelf life, so you can keep them on hand for the following year.

Easter Basket and Bunnies Cupcakes

  2 cups granulated sugar

1¾ cups all-purpose flour

  ¾ cup HERSHEY'S Cocoa or HERSHEY'S SPECIAL DARK® Cocoa

1½ teaspoons baking powder

1½ teaspoons baking soda

  1 teaspoon salt

  2 eggs

  1 cup milk

  ½ cup vegetable oil

  2 teaspoons vanilla extract

  1 cup boiling water

    CREAMY VANILLA FROSTING (recipe follows)

    Green, red and yellow food color

3¾ cups MOUNDS® Sweetened Coconut Flakes, divided and tinted*

    Suggested garnishes (marshmallows, HERSHEY'S MINI KISSES® Brand Milk Chocolates, licorice, jelly beans)

*To tint coconut: Combine ¾ teaspoon water with several drops green food color in small bowl. Stir in 1¼ cups coconut. Toss with fork until evenly tinted. Repeat with red and yellow food color and remaining coconut.

1. Heat oven to 350°F. Line muffin cups (2½ inches in diameter) with paper bake cups.

2. Stir together granulated sugar, flour, cocoa, baking powder, baking soda and salt in large bowl. Add eggs, milk, oil and vanilla; beat with electric mixer at medium speed 2 minutes. Stir in boiling water (batter will be thin). Fill muffin cups two-thirds full with batter.

3. Bake 22 to 25 minutes or until wooden pick inserted in center comes out clean. Cool completely. Prepare Creamy Vanilla Frosting; frost cupcakes. Immediately press desired color tinted coconut onto each cupcake. Garnish as desired to resemble Easter basket or bunny. *Makes 33 cupcakes*

Creamy Vanilla Frosting: Beat ⅓ cup softened butter or margarine in medium bowl. Add 1 cup powdered sugar and 1½ teaspoons vanilla extract; beat well. Add 2½ cups powdered sugar alternately with ¼ cup milk, beating to spreading consistency. Makes about 2 cups frosting.

Coconut Mother's Day Cake

1 package (about 18 ounces) white cake mix
1 can (about 13 ounces) light coconut milk
4 egg whites
1 container (16 ounces) vanilla frosting
2 cups flaked coconut
   Purple food coloring paste
   Edible flowers (optional)

1. Preheat oven to 350°F. Grease two 8-inch round cake pans; line with parchment paper.

2. Beat cake mix, coconut milk and egg whites in large bowl with electric mixer at low speed 30 seconds. Beat at medium-low speed 2 minutes or until well blended. Divide batter evenly between prepared pans.

3. Bake 40 to 45 minutes or until toothpick inserted into centers comes out clean. Cool cakes 10 minutes in pans on wire racks. Remove to racks; cool completely.

4. Place one cake layer on serving platter; frost top with vanilla frosting. Top with remaining layer; frost side and top of cake with remaining frosting.

5. Place coconut in large resealable food storage bag; add small amount of food coloring. Seal bag; knead until coconut is evenly tinted. Press coconut into frosting on side of cake. Garnish with edible flowers.

Makes 10 servings

Graduation Party Cupcakes

   1 package (about 18 ounces) white cake mix
1¼ cups water
  ⅓ cup vegetable oil
  3 egg whites
   Food coloring, in coordinating school colors
  1 container (16 ounces) white frosting
22 chocolate squares
   Gummy candy strips, in coordinating school colors
22 mini candy-coated chocolate pieces, in coordinating school colors

1. Preheat oven to 325°F. Line 22 standard (2½-inch) muffin cups with paper baking cups.

2. Beat cake mix, water, oil and egg whites in large bowl with electric mixer at medium speed 2 minutes or until blended. (Batter will be slightly lumpy.) Add food coloring to match one school color. Pour batter into prepared muffin cups, filling two-thirds full.

3. Bake 17 to 20 minutes or until toothpick inserted into centers comes out clean. Cool cupcakes 10 minutes in pans on wire racks. Remove to racks; cool completely.

4. Tint frosting with alternate food coloring. Frost cupcakes.

5. Place chocolate square on top of cupcake. Place small dab of frosting in center of square to attach candy strips for tassel and chocolate piece for button.

Makes 22 cupcakes

Liberty's Torches

1 package (about 18 ounces) cake mix, any flavor, plus ingredients to prepare mix

24 flat-bottomed ice cream cones

1 container (16 ounces) white frosting

Yellow food coloring

24 red, yellow and orange chewy fruit roll-ups

1. Preheat oven to 350°F. Stand ice cream cones in 13×9-inch pan or place cones in muffin cups.

2. Prepare cake mix according to package directions. Fill each cone with 2½ tablespoons batter. Bake 30 minutes or until toothpick inserted into centers comes out clean. Remove cones to wire rack; cool completely.

3. Tint frosting yellow. Frost cupcakes. Cut pointy flames from fruit roll-ups using kitchen scissors or sharp knife. Fold or roll flames to stand upright; arrange on cupcakes before frosting sets.   *Makes 24 cupcakes*

Stars and Stripes Cupcakes

42 cupcakes, any flavor

2 containers (16 ounces each) vanilla frosting

Fresh blueberries

Fresh strawberries, stemmed and halved

1. Frost cupcakes.

2. Top 9 cupcakes with blueberries. Decorate remaining cupcakes with strawberry halves.

3. Arrange cupcakes on large rectangular tray to form United States flag. Place blueberry-topped cupcakes in upper left corner and strawberry-topped cupcakes in rows to resemble red and white stripes of flag.

Makes 42 cupcakes

Fun in the Sun Cake

2 packages (about 18 ounces each) carrot cake mix, plus ingredients to prepare mix

1 jar (18 ounces) pineapple preserves

2 containers (16 ounces each) cream cheese frosting

Raw sugar

Shell-shaped candies

Fruit leather, various colors

Paper umbrella

Large round peppermint candy or jawbreaker

8 candy spearmint leaves

Wire

2 cream-filled pirouette cookies

1. Prepare cake mix and bake in two 10-inch round cake pans and two 8-inch round cake pans according to package directions. Cool 15 minutes in pans on wire racks. Remove to racks; cool completely. Trim tops of cakes to make level.

2. Warm preserves in microwave just until spreadable. Place one 10-inch cake layer on serving platter; spread top with half of preserves. Top with other 10-inch cake layer; spread some of the frosting over top. Place one 8-inch cake layer on top; spread top with remaining preserves. Top with remaining cake layer. Frost entire cake with remaining frosting.

3. Pat raw sugar all over cake to resemble sand. Add shell candies around base of cake and on top of both tiers. To make beach towel, piece together thin strips of colored fruit leather. Fringe ends with scissors, if desired. Place beach towel on top of cake and add paper umbrella. Place round peppermint or jawbreaker at towel's edge for beach ball.

4. To make palm trees, roll out spearmint leaves between sheets of waxed paper until very thin. Fringe edges with scissors. Cut wire into four 5-inch lengths. Pierce one wire through each pirouette cookie about ½ inch from one end. Pierce second wire at right angle to first wire to form a cross. Gently lay spearmint leaves on wires and press gently to adhere. Bend wires to get desired palm tree effect. Poke two holes into cake top with handle of spoon and carefully insert palm trees. *Makes 20 servings*

Note: Remove wire palm trees before serving.

Jack-O'-Lantern

Buttercream Frosting (page 22)
Orange, green and brown food coloring
2 **(10-inch) bundt cakes**
Base Frosting (page 23, optional)
1 **ice cream wafer cone**
Candy corn

1. Prepare 2 recipes Buttercream Frosting. Tint 4½ cups frosting orange, ½ cup dark green and ¼ cup dark brown.

2. Trim flat sides of cakes. Place one cake on large platter, flat-side up. Frost top of cake with some of the orange frosting. Place second cake, flat-side down, over frosting.

3. Frost entire cake with Base Frosting to seal in crumbs, if desired. Frost entire cake with remaining orange frosting.

4. Frost ice cream cone with green frosting. Place upside-down in center of cake to form stem. Touch up frosting, if necessary.

5. Using medium writing tip and brown frosting, pipe eyes and mouth. Arrange candy corn for teeth as shown in photo. Slice and serve top cake first, then bottom. *Makes 36 to 40 servings*

Tip: A fall birthday is the perfect opportunity for a party with a Halloween theme. Create scary decorations like spiderwebs and bats hanging from the ceiling and perhaps a coffin or graveyard scene. Turn down the lights and play a tape of scary sounds to add to the spooky atmosphere. Costumes are, of course, required but you may want to make masks as part of the party. Provide a plain mask for each child and supply plenty of paints, markers, construction paper, crepe paper, fabric, yarn and glitter. Stickers are also an easy way to decorate. Awards can be given for the scariest, prettiest or most creative—just be sure every child wins something.

Sparkling Tree Cakes

    1 package (2-layer size) yellow cake mix
    ¼ teaspoon green food coloring
    1 package (8 ounces) PHILADELPHIA® Cream Cheese, softened
    1 cup powdered sugar
 1½ cups thawed COOL WHIP® Whipped Topping
  16 peppermint sticks (3 inches each)
    ½ cup BAKER'S ANGEL FLAKE® Coconut
    2 squares BAKER'S® Semi-Sweet Baking Chocolate, chopped
    ¼ cup PLANTERS® Dry Roasted Peanuts, chopped
        Assorted Christmas candies and colored sugar

PREHEAT oven to 350°F. Grease and flour 2 (9-inch) round cake pans; set aside. Prepare cake batter as directed on package; tint with food coloring. Pour evenly into prepared pans.

BAKE as directed on package. Cool in pans 10 minutes; remove to wire racks. Cool completely.

BEAT cream cheese and powdered sugar with electric mixer on medium speed until well blended. Stir in whipped topping with wire whisk. Spread onto tops and sides of cakes.

CUT each cake into 8 wedges to resemble Christmas trees. Insert peppermint stick into curved side of each cake for the tree trunk. Decorate with remaining ingredients. Store in refrigerator.   *Makes 16 servings, 1 tree each*

Size-Wise: With their built-in portion control, these cakes make great holiday treats!

Let it Snow

2 (9-inch) round cake layers

2 (10-inch) round cake boards, taped together and covered, or large tray

1½ cups prepared white frosting or Buttercream Frosting (page 22)

½ cup prepared chocolate frosting or Chocolate Buttercream Frosting (page 34)

Assorted gumdrops

1 sugar ice cream cone, cut in half crosswise

Red pull-apart licorice twists

1. Trim tops of cake layers to make level. Cut off small piece from one side of each cake layer to form flat edge (so layers will fit together as shown in photo).

2. Place one cake layer as bottom half of snowman on prepared cake board. Using diagram as guide, draw pattern for snowman's head (with hat) on 9-inch circle of waxed paper. Cut out pattern; use to cut out head from second cake layer. Place snowman's head on cake board; attach flat edges of cake layers with small amount of white frosting.

3. Frost hat with chocolate frosting. Frost remaining cake with white frosting.

4. Decorate snowman with assorted gumdrops and ice cream cone nose as shown in photo. Arrange licorice to resemble hatband and scarf as shown in photo. *Makes 16 to 18 servings*

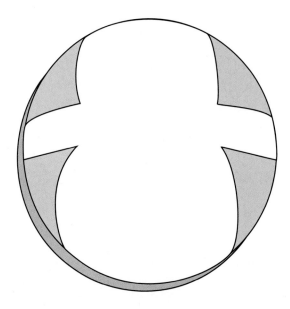

CELEBRATION CLASSICS

····

Surprise Package Cupcakes

1 package (about 18 ounces) cake mix, any flavor, plus ingredients to prepare mix

Food coloring (optional)

1 container (16 ounces) vanilla frosting

1 tube (4¼ ounces) white decorating icing

72 chewy fruit squares

Colored decors

1. Preheat oven to 350°F. Line 24 standard (2½-inch) muffin cups with paper baking cups or spray with nonstick cooking spray.

2. Prepare cake mix and bake in prepared muffin cups according to package directions. Cool cupcakes 15 minutes in pans on wire racks. Remove to racks; cool completely.

3. Tint frosting with food coloring, if desired. Frost cupcakes.

4. Use icing to pipe ribbons on fruit squares to resemble wrapped presents. Place 3 candy presents on each cupcake. Decorate with decors.

Makes 24 cupcakes

Chocolate Bar Cake

5 HERSHEY'S Milk Chocolate Bars (1.55 ounces each), broken into pieces
½ cup (1 stick) butter or margarine, softened
1 cup boiling water
2 cups all-purpose flour
1½ cups sugar
½ cup HERSHEY'S Cocoa
2 teaspoons baking soda
1 teaspoon salt
2 eggs
½ cup dairy sour cream
1 teaspoon vanilla extract
VANILLA GLAZE (recipe follows)
Additional HERSHEY'S Milk Chocolate Bar (1.55 ounces), (optional)

1. Heat oven to 350°F. Grease and flour 12-cup fluted tube pan.

2. Stir together chocolate bar pieces, butter and water in small bowl until chocolate is melted. Stir together flour, sugar, cocoa, baking soda and salt in large bowl; gradually add chocolate mixture, beating on medium speed of mixer until well blended. Add eggs, sour cream and vanilla; blend well. Beat 1 minute. Pour batter into prepared pan.

3. Bake 50 to 55 minutes or until wooden pick inserted in center comes out clean. Cool 10 minutes; remove from pan to wire rack. Cool completely. Prepare Vanilla Glaze; drizzle over cake. Cut additional chocolate bar into small pieces; decorate top of cake, if desired. *Makes 10 to 12 servings*

Vanilla Glaze

¼ cup (½ stick) butter or margarine
2 cups powdered sugar
2 tablespoons hot water
1 teaspoon vanilla extract

Place butter in medium microwave-safe bowl. Microwave at MEDIUM (50%) 30 seconds or until melted. Gradually stir in powdered sugar, water and vanilla; beat with whisk until smooth and slightly thickened. Add additional water, 1 teaspoon at a time, if needed.

Lemon-Orange Party Cake

    1 package (about 18 ounces) yellow cake mix with pudding in the mix
1¼ cups plus 5 tablespoons orange juice, divided
    3 eggs
   ⅓ cup vegetable oil
    2 tablespoons grated orange peel
5½ cups sifted powdered sugar, divided
   ⅓ cup lemon juice
   ⅓ cup butter, softened
    Colored sprinkles
 20 candy fruit slices

1. Preheat oven to 350°F. Lightly grease 13×9-inch baking pan.

2. Beat cake mix, 1¼ cups orange juice, eggs, oil and orange peel in large bowl with electric mixer at low speed 1 minute or until blended. Beat at medium speed 1 to 2 minutes or until smooth. Spread in prepared pan.

3. Bake 33 to 38 minutes or until toothpick inserted into center comes out clean. Meanwhile, combine 1 cup powdered sugar and lemon juice in small bowl; stir until smooth.

4. Pierce top of warm cake with large fork or wooden skewer at ½-inch intervals. Slowly drizzle lemon glaze over warm cake. Cool completely.

5. Beat remaining 4½ cups powdered sugar and butter in large bowl with electric mixer at low speed until blended. Beat in enough remaining orange juice to reach spreading consistency. Spread frosting over cooled cake. Decorate top of cake with sprinkles and candy fruit slices.

Makes 20 servings

Flourless Chocolate Torte

1¼ cups (2½ sticks) butter

¾ cup HERSHEY'S Cocoa

2 cups sugar, divided

6 eggs, separated

¼ cup water

1 teaspoon vanilla extract

1 cup blanched sliced almonds, toasted and ground*

½ cup plain dry bread crumbs

MOCHA CREAM (recipe follows)

To toast almonds: Heat oven to 350°F. Place almonds in single layer in shallow baking pan. Bake 7 to 8 minutes, stirring occasionally, until light brown. Cool.

1. Heat oven to 350°F. Grease and flour 9-inch springform pan. Melt butter in saucepan over low heat. Add cocoa and 1½ cups sugar; stir until smooth. Cool to room temperature.

2. Beat egg yolks in large bowl until thick. Gradually beat in chocolate mixture; stir in water and vanilla. Combine ground almonds and bread crumbs; stir into chocolate mixture.

3. Beat egg whites until foamy; gradually add remaining ½ cup sugar, beating until soft peaks form. Fold about one-third of egg whites into chocolate. Fold chocolate into remaining egg whites. Pour into prepared pan.

4. Bake 50 to 60 minutes or until wooden pick inserted in center comes out clean. Cool 10 minutes. Loosen cake from side of pan; remove pan. Cool completely. Spread Mocha Cream over top. Sift with cocoa just before serving. Store covered in refrigerator.   *Makes 10 servings*

Mocha Cream: Combine 1 cup (½ pint) cold whipping cream, 2 tablespoons powdered sugar, 1½ teaspoons powdered instant coffee dissolved in 1 teaspoon water, and ½ teaspoon vanilla extract in medium bowl; beat until stiff. Makes about 2 cups.

Apricot Cream Cake

Cake

    1 package DUNCAN HINES® Moist Deluxe® Classic Yellow Cake Mix

    1 jar (18 ounces) apricot preserves, divided

Frosting

    1 package (4-serving size) vanilla-flavor instant pudding and pie filling mix

    ¾ cup milk

    1½ cups whipping cream, chilled

    ¼ cup toasted flaked coconut, for garnish

    Apricot halves and mint leaves, for garnish

1. Preheat oven to 350°F. Grease and flour two 9-inch round cake pans.

2. For cake, prepare, bake and cool cake following package directions for basic recipe.

3. To assemble, split each cake layer in half horizontally. Reserve 1 tablespoon preserves. Place one split cake layer on serving plate. Spread one-third remaining preserves on top. Repeat with remaining layers and preserves, leaving top plain.

4. For frosting, prepare pudding mix as directed on package, using ¾ cup milk. Beat whipping cream until stiff in large bowl. Fold whipped cream into pudding. Spread on sides and top of cake. Garnish with coconut, apricot halves and mint leaves. Warm reserved 1 tablespoon preserves to glaze apricot halves. Refrigerate until ready to serve. *Makes 12 to 16 servings*

Tip: You can substitute 3 cups thawed frozen nondairy whipped topping for the whipping cream.

Rich Chocolate Cake with Creamy Peanut Butter Milk Chocolate Frosting

Cake

- 2 cups all-purpose flour
- 1¾ cups granulated sugar
- ⅔ cup NESTLÉ® TOLL HOUSE® Baking Cocoa
- 1½ teaspoons baking powder
- 1½ teaspoons baking soda
- ½ teaspoon salt
- 1 cup milk
- 1 cup water
- ½ cup vegetable oil
- 2 eggs
- 2 teaspoons vanilla extract
- 1⅔ cups (11-ounce package) NESTLÉ® TOLL HOUSE® Peanut Butter & Milk Chocolate Morsels, divided

Creamy Peanut Butter Milk Chocolate Frosting

- 1 package (8 ounces) cream cheese, softened
- 1 teaspoon vanilla extract
- ⅛ teaspoon salt
- 3 cups powdered sugar

Garnish

- 1 bar (2 ounces total) NESTLÉ® TOLL HOUSE® Semi-Sweet Chocolate Baking Bar, made into curls (see Tip)

For Cake

PREHEAT oven to 350°F. Grease and flour two 9-inch-round cake pans.

COMBINE flour, granulated sugar, cocoa, baking powder, baking soda and salt in large mixer bowl. Add milk, water, vegetable oil, eggs and vanilla extract; blend until moistened. Beat for 2 minutes (batter will be thin). Pour into prepared pans. Sprinkle ⅓ *cup* morsels over each cake layer.

BAKE for 25 to 30 minutes or until wooden pick inserted in center comes out clean. Cool in pans on wire racks for 10 minutes; remove to wire racks to cool completely. Frost with Creamy Peanut Butter Milk Chocolate Frosting between layers and on top and side of cake. Garnish with chocolate curls before serving.

For Creamy Peanut Butter Milk Chocolate Frosting

MICROWAVE *remaining* morsels in small, uncovered, microwave-safe bowl on MEDIUM-HIGH (70%) power for 1 minute. STIR. Morsels may retain some of their original shape. If necessary, microwave at additional 10- to 15-second intervals, stirring just until morsels are melted. Beat cream cheese, melted morsels, vanilla extract and salt in small mixer bowl until light and fluffy. Gradually beat in powdered sugar.   *Makes 10 to 12 servings*

Tip: To make chocolate curls, carefully draw a vegetable peeler across a bar of NESTLÉ® TOLL HOUSE® Semi-Sweet Chocolate. Vary the width of your curls by using different sides of the chocolate bar.

Red Velvet Cake

2 packages (about 18 ounces each) white cake mix
2 tablespoons cocoa powder (optional)
2 teaspoons baking soda
3 cups buttermilk
4 eggs
2 bottles (1 ounce each) red food coloring
2 containers (16 ounces each) cream cheese frosting

1. Preheat oven to 350°F. Grease and flour four 9-inch round cake pans.

2. Combine cake mixes, cocoa powder, if desired, and baking soda in large bowl. Add buttermilk, eggs and food coloring; beat with electric mixer at low speed until moistened. Beat at high speed 2 minutes.

3. Pour batter into prepared pans. Bake 30 to 35 minutes or until toothpick inserted into centers comes out clean. Cool 10 minutes in pans on wire racks. Remove to racks; cool completely.

4. Place one cake layer on serving plate; spread with frosting. Repeat with second and third cake layers. Top with fourth cake layer; frost top and side of cake.

Makes 16 servings

Red Velvet Cake has been an American favorite for decades. It has a mild chocolate flavor from the cocoa powder and a moist texture that comes from the addition of buttermilk.

Acknowledgments

The publisher would like to thank the companies listed
below for the use of their recipes and photographs
in this publication.

Duncan Hines® and Moist Deluxe® are registered trademarks
of Pinnacle Foods Corp.

The Hershey Company

© 2009 Kraft Foods, KRAFT, KRAFT Hexagon Logo,
PHILADELPHIA AND PHILADELPHIA Logo are registered
trademarks of Kraft Foods Holdings, Inc. All rights reserved.

Nestlé USA

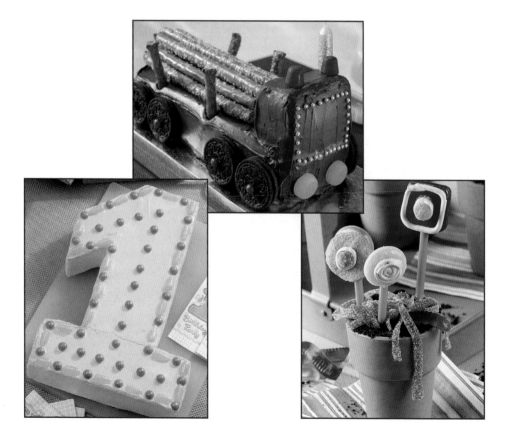

Index

METRIC CONVERSION CHART

VOLUME MEASUREMENTS (dry)

1/8 teaspoon = 0.5 mL
1/4 teaspoon = 1 mL
1/2 teaspoon = 2 mL
3/4 teaspoon = 4 mL
1 teaspoon = 5 mL
1 tablespoon = 15 mL
2 tablespoons = 30 mL
1/4 cup = 60 mL
1/3 cup = 75 mL
1/2 cup = 125 mL
2/3 cup = 150 mL
3/4 cup = 175 mL
1 cup = 250 mL
2 cups = 1 pint = 500 mL
3 cups = 750 mL
4 cups = 1 quart = 1 L

VOLUME MEASUREMENTS (fluid)

1 fluid ounce (2 tablespoons) = 30 mL
4 fluid ounces (1/2 cup) = 125 mL
8 fluid ounces (1 cup) = 250 mL
12 fluid ounces (1 1/2 cups) = 375 mL
16 fluid ounces (2 cups) = 500 mL

WEIGHTS (mass)

1/2 ounce = 15 g
1 ounce = 30 g
3 ounces = 90 g
4 ounces = 120 g
8 ounces = 225 g
10 ounces = 285 g
12 ounces = 360 g
16 ounces = 1 pound = 450 g

DIMENSIONS

1/16 inch = 2 mm
1/8 inch = 3 mm
1/4 inch = 6 mm
1/2 inch = 1.5 cm
3/4 inch = 2 cm
1 inch = 2.5 cm

OVEN TEMPERATURES

250°F = 120°C
275°F = 140°C
300°F = 150°C
325°F = 160°C
350°F = 180°C
375°F = 190°C
400°F = 200°C
425°F = 220°C
450°F = 230°C

BAKING PAN SIZES

Utensil	Size in Inches/Quarts	Metric Volume	Size in Centimeters
Baking or Cake Pan (square or rectangular)	8×8×2	2 L	20×20×5
	9×9×2	2.5 L	23×23×5
	12×8×2	3 L	30×20×5
	13×9×2	3.5 L	33×23×5
Loaf Pan	8×4×3	1.5 L	20×10×7
	9×5×3	2 L	23×13×7
Round Layer Cake Pan	8×1½	1.2 L	20×4
	9×1½	1.5 L	23×4
Pie Plate	8×1¼	750 mL	20×3
	9×1¼	1 L	23×3
Baking Dish or Casserole	1 quart	1 L	—
	1½ quart	1.5 L	—
	2 quart	2 L	—